God's Trustees

Managing All of Life and Life's Resources for God's Purposes!

Gerhard C. "Mike" Michael, Jr.
and
David S. Belasic

Concordia Publishing House

Edited by Thomas J. Doyle

1 2 3 4 5 6 7 8 9 10   10 09 08 07 06 05 04 03 02 01

Contents

Foreword

"Stewardship . . . that's about budgets and fund-raising. Right?"

Few biblical teachings are more misunderstood than stewardship. Although stewardship education is not easy, it is vitally important for the ministry of God's church. This booklet will assist followers of Jesus to expand their understanding of both individual and group stewardship. Use it in a variety of settings, with choices being made about the amount of discussion time allotted for each section. The desire is that participants will grow in the awareness of the joyous privilege of being God's trustees!

To get the most out of these studies, consider the following:

1. The material is heavily biblical in character. There are many, many Bible references for group leaders and participants to read and consider. However, the application of the material is practical. Participants will see God's blessings at work personally *and* in congregational life.

2. Adults most frequently learn from and with each other. Therefore, lecture is not always the best teaching method. The Holy Spirit will bless the sharing of God's Word as His people learn from it with one another. Discussion invites challenge. Each session can promote lasting biblical insights, thoughtful reflections, and ideas for action. This is more than an information course. The desired outcome is one of Christlike spiritual growth, maturity, and transformation of life in attitude and action (Philippians 2:4–11; Romans 12:1–2).

3. The materials can be presented so that the reality of being God's trustee touches on *all* of life, including, but not limited to, the use of "time, talent, and treasure" for the sake of the institutional church. This study will challenge both long-time members of the church and new Christians to consider God's purposes for life and the privileged part that each Christian trustee plays in God's plan (Jeremiah 29:11).

4. In Christ, God calls us to see stewardship as the very essence of faith and life. It is all-encompassing. It flavors and penetrates the whole loaf of life, not just one slice. The miracle—the mystery of Christ's grace—is that He continues to give redeemed people the honor, the trust, of being instruments of His hope and blessing . . . hence the title, *God's Trustees!*

5. Though each session may be used for a sixty or ninety minute class, some leaders and groups may choose to spend two or three times that amount of time on each of the sessions! Much will depend on searching the Scriptures and sharing together!

We want to help believers in Christ, members of the church, find new *satisfaction*, *meaning*, and *enjoyment* in being and seeing themselves as God's stewards—honored and chosen trustees of life and all of life's resources (2 Corinthians 5:14–15)! May our Lord bless your use of these materials as you equip *God's Trustees!*

"Mike" and David

WOW!
God Trusts Me!

In this session we will endeavor to

discover what it means to be God's steward;
experience a sense of awe over the fact
that God trusts us to be His stewards;
begin to see all of life as an expression
of our stewardship.

Opening Prayer

Psalm 8

O Lord God, Father, Son, and Holy Spirit—You amaze us.
You have given us a privileged position in Your creation.
Through the study and discussion we begin today, help each of
us learn again to fulfill the trust You have given to us. In Jesus'
name and for His sake we pray. Amen.

Seeking Wisdom . . .

The Old Testament story of Joseph gives us an example of
a steward carrying out his stewardship, serving an owner and
many others. Together, scan the story of Joseph in Genesis 39,
especially verses 4–6 and 19–23. Identify the verses indicating
that (1) Joseph was the chosen steward/manager, (2) he had freedom to manage the household for Potiphar, (3) he was trusted,
(4) he was accountable to his boss, and (5) he was condemned
and removed from his stewardship because he was judged
unfaithful (although unjustly).

Another portion of Scripture that guides our study of being

God's steward is Luke 12:42–48. Scan the context, the previous few paragraphs, and discuss the following:

1. What does the master expect his servants to be doing in his absence? Why has the master placed the servant/steward in charge?

2. Since the master is not present, what does the servant/steward enjoy?

3. What will happen when the master returns?

4. Summarize the key points we learn about being God's stewards from this teaching of Jesus.

Reflecting . . .

We have entitled this course *God's Trustees* to highlight the truth that "trust" is at the heart of stewardship. A steward is someone who has been entrusted with the property or person of another. He/she is asked to provide proper care (to manage) on behalf of the other person (the owner).

Elected government officials have a stewardship (a trust) to exercise. They are to manage the affairs of state for us, the voters. When elections are held, the people in office are held accountable for their stewardship. Based on this, they may be reelected or not.

5. Identify a list of additional contemporary examples of stewardship—someone entrusting something or someone to the care of another.

6. Identify the stewardship *you* have been given to exercise. List as many examples as you can in a few minutes. These might include time, family member, job, friend, citizen, taxpayer, and so on.

7. After reflecting, share with the entire group those areas of stewardship that you believe currently impact others the most and one or two that have a long-range impact. Write them here.

Applying . . . Living What We Believe . . .

The stewardship we exercise at work, at home, in the community, and in the church is really a stewardship from God. In each of these arenas we are privileged to demonstrate and live out the fact that we have been placed here by God to live and act as a manager, a trustee, for Him. It is a life-directing discovery to realize that *God really trusts me* to make decisions, to manage things, to take care of people and things for Him.

8. In a moment we will look at biblical evidence that God trusts us with His work. Right now, as a group, identify (share/list) the evidence that people trust you in ordinary daily relationships.

9. When do you sense that your spouse, parent, child, and/or friend trusts you? How does that affect the way you carry out your responsibilities, your stewardship of that situation?

10. How do you know that your boss trusts you? How does her/his confidence affect your performance?

11. How do children know that their parents trust them? How might that affect their behavior?

12. A major question in life is this: How do you know that God really trusts you to be His steward, a manager, a trustee? This is a key concern, since the person who senses that he is trusted normally seeks to live up to the other person's trust. He does not want to let the other person down. The trustee of a child's trust fund, who was personally selected by the child's parent because he was a trusted family friend, will more likely want to manage that trust fund well because of the trust he enjoys. Trust inspires responsibility. So how do you know that God trusts you? What has God done to encourage you to faithfully exercise the trust He has given you?

13. Consider the following Bible passages as you gain insight for living as God's trustee.

Matthew 28:18–20	John 3:14–17
John 15:12–17	1 Corinthians 1:26–31
2 Corinthians 5:14–15	Ephesians 2:11–16
1 Peter 2:9–12	

In the group, share some of your thoughts on what God is saying to you, His beloved trustee!

At the dinner table a little boy says, "Dad, I just had an idea. Let's build a birdhouse tonight just for the fun of it." Dad agrees. The little boy gets some wood from the garage, but it's the wrong piece of wood for a birdhouse. But since they are doing this together for the fun of it, they mark the lines and use the board. Dad turns on the power saw and the boy is about to push the board across the whirling blade, when Dad calls, "Hold on a minute. This could be dangerous. Let me help you." He puts his hand over the boy's hand and proceeds to cut out the pieces for the birdhouse. The little boy wiggles a bit so some of the pieces do not match perfectly. If Dad wanted to build a perfect birdhouse, he could have set the boy on a stool just to watch while he built it. *That would have destroyed the joy of the partnership!*

They put the birdhouse together, and the boy gets out the blue and gold paint cans. He spills a few drops on the paper, but completes the paint job and looks at the new birdhouse with great admiration.

The next day the boy is really excited as he heads to school with the birdhouse. One of his classmates says, "Where did you get that neat birdhouse?" He answers proudly, "My Dad and I built it. We do things like this all the time—just for the fun of it!"

In the days ahead, think of the partnership we have as God's stewards. Remember how He guides our hands and our lives and brings joy to the lives of others. God in Christ has chosen to draw a world of people back to Himself through His Son's death on the cross. Each one of us, baptized, blessed, in the name of Christ becomes a co-worker, a trustee, in His plan. We are not slaves driven by a self-serving God, but rather we are committed partners in our heavenly Father's desire to help people here and everywhere live a life with meaning and purpose.

The authors of this material believe that "*the purpose of life . . . (for all of us who are baptized in the name of the triune God) . . . is to make a contribution to others in the name of Jesus Christ.*" It's how we see our mission as God's trustees.

14. How do you describe your mission?

Summarizing . . .

- God shows His love for me in Jesus Christ, in Baptism, in Scripture, in Holy Communion, in His church, by calling me to be His child even though I do not deserve it.
- God shows He trusts me by entrusting me with His work. He calls me to manage my God-given life and life's resources to fulfill His purposes.
- God shows He trusts me by not treating me as a puppet on a string. He enables me to make decisions as His steward, even to make mistakes.
- God picks me up when I fall and disappoint Him as His trustee. His restoring love in Christ renews my desire to be His steward each new day.

Closing Prayer

Heavenly Father, maker and owner of all that exists, You really trust me. I thank You, God! In all the days of my life, help me to reflect my trust in You by seeking Your wisdom and becoming a wise and faithful manager of all You have entrusted to me. I pray in the name of Jesus, the One who redeemed me to be Your steward. Amen.

What's All in the Bag God Has Given Me?!

In this session we will endeavor to

*become more aware of the many resources
God entrusts to us;
receive with thanksgiving the resources
God has given to us;
grow in developing, using, and managing
the resources entrusted to us.*

Opening Prayer

Psalm 1

*O Lord God, Father, Son, and Holy Spirit—You give us all
we are and have. Help us again today to discover anew the gifts
You have given. Help us to receive them with thanksgiving.
Help us to use the gifts You provide so that others You put into
our lives may be blessed. Help us in everything we manage as
Your trustees to honor and glorify You. In Jesus' name we pray.
Amen.*

Seeking Wisdom . . .

In our previous session we learned from the Bible that trust
is at the heart of our stewardship. God trusts us to be managers,
trustees, for Him. He has created us to be His people and
charges us to represent Him (Genesis 1:26–28). The Lord Jesus
Christ redeemed us from our sin, our self-centeredness, by His

life, death, and resurrection. Until He returns, He has commissioned us to spread the Word of His life-giving, life-changing work and share His love with all whose lives we can touch in our wayward world. This is our privilege, our trusteeship, our stewardship.

The great thing about this privilege is that our Lord provides a wide variety of the resources we need to live as His trustees. He passes out His gifts in different forms and degrees. Each of us is challenged to discover, develop, and deploy the gifts He has entrusted to us . . . and to do it for the common good . . . in the name of the Owner and Redeemer of us all!

Studying the Scripture together under the guidance of the Holy Spirit, we can help one another grow to recognize our gifts, receive them with thanksgiving, and use them willingly as God's people. A parable of Jesus that illustrates the nature of Christian stewardship is in Matthew 25:14–30. Please read it aloud. Note the specific verses for some of the following points:

- The owner entrusted property to his servants to manage for him in his absence.
- Their stewardship included the freedom to make responsible decisions for the owner.
- Accountability was required when the owner returned.
- The owner commended the faithful servants and rejected the faithless servant.

15. For a few minutes, focus on verse 15, to "each according to his ability." What does this say about expectations? What light does it cast on the parable (an earthly story with a heavenly meaning)?

16. Examine 1 Peter 4:7–11, especially focusing on verses 10–11. Then read 1 Corinthians 12:4–11 (especially note verse 7) as you consider the words of Jesus. What do Peter and Paul

add to our understanding of the use of God-given gifts, skills, and resources?

17. Who determines what you get? How much you get? How does the language of "grace" and "gift" help us look at our stewardship in a new way? What is that way? How do these parts of the Bible foster a sense of "teamwork" and of being the "body of Christ," the church? How is our understanding of "stewardship" and "trusteeship" affected as we realize they are gifts given to us by God?

Reflecting . . .

For a few minutes, reflect on some of the resources God has provided us.

18. Begin with your body. Read Psalm 139:14. Reflect on this marvelous system God has given. Is there anything humans have made that can match it? Look up 2 Corinthians 12:9–10 and put into your own words how Paul is led to handle his own bodily weaknesses. What does that say about stewardship?

19. In conjunction with our bodies, please consider the talents, skills, abilities, and interests God has given each one of us. Make a list of what you feel are the gifts God has given you. Since God gives them, we can be realistic in identifying them. The gifts that I believe God has given me include:

20. Share with the group the ones on the list you feel quite positive about or the ones you have questions about.

21. Continue with the creation around you. Read Genesis 1:29. Reflect on the variety God has put into creation for us to enjoy! Think about the air, the water, the land, the parks, the colors, the change of seasons. What aspects of creation do you enjoy most?

22. Sometimes religious people denigrate the material side of life. Look at Paul's words in 1 Timothy 4:4–5. What is the appropriate attitude he teaches? What can also help us to enjoy God's goodness while not having our enjoyment ruined by greed? Consider 1 Timothy 6:6–10 and 17–19.

Think about the things in one of your closets or storage areas, and list the items you were privileged to enjoy . . . and especially recall the relationships they represent! They are gifts of God!

23. Reflect on the gift of people. Take a moment to list the names of five people whose care and friendship have enriched your life.

24. Showing thankfulness to others is a part of being God's trustee. Make time this week to find a way to express your gratitude to one or two people who have enriched your life. Write your plans here:

25. Consider the gift of the Gospel: God's forgiving, empowering, eternal life–giving love through His Son, Jesus Christ! What has Jesus done for you? Describe it in your own words. Share a few of your thoughts and feelings about Him with the group.

26. Reflect on how the following resources, gifts of God to be used and enjoyed, can help us live more meaningfully and significantly as God's trustees, "stewards of the Gospel"!

Holy Baptism (Matthew 28:16–20; Romans 6:1–11; Galatians 3:26–29 and 4:4–7)

Holy Communion (Matthew 26:26–29; 1 Corinthians 10:16–22)

God's family, the church, the body of Christ (Romans 12:4–5; 1 Corinthians 12:12–14, 27)

The Word of God (John 1:14–18; Isaiah 55:6–11; Romans 1:16–17; 1 Corinthians 1:18–25)

The forgiveness of sin (John 8:1–11 and 31–36; Luke 15:11–24)

27. As God's steward, which of these resources is the most meaningful to you at this time in your life? Which of them do you think you will need to be more aware of in the future?

Each of us gets one day at a time—sixty minutes in an

hour, twenty-four hours in a day! Our stewardship of time is vital—a nonrenewable resource. Time can fly or drag. No matter how we use it, it is a gift of God. Regular time for Scripture reading and prayer can mightily influence how we use the rest of our time.

28. Do you know of individuals who tithe (give ten percent) of their time to God each day or week in a direct way? What do they do? What are they like? Share with each other ways in which you might improve your stewardship of time.

Applying . . . Living What We Believe . . .

29. From the previous section, select two items that you will endeavor to apply to your life as God's trustee in the coming weeks, and tell the group what you would like to do.

30. Which of the gifts God has given to you might bring the greatest satisfaction to your life as you apply it in the next twelve months?

Until Next Time . . .

Read Psalm 1 each day. Who are the "models" of the

"blessed" ones that God has put into your life? As you pray Psalm 1 this week, thank God for the "models" in your life, for what they mean or have meant to you. Ask God to raise up an increasing number of "models" for young stewards in your congregation and community.

Summarizing . . .

- God places a wide variety of resources in my bag . . . to be used as His steward.
- God gives gifts "for the common good" . . . and they are developed with help from others.
- "What I am is God's gift to me. What I become is my response to God." I'm God's steward.

Closing Prayer

Heavenly Father, giver of all gifts, maker and owner of all that exists, enable me to live with an attitude of gratitude every day. Help me to continually discover, develop, and deploy the gifts You have entrusted to me. Help me to make the most of the time You give me in this world, and help us all to confess, "We give You but Your own, in any gifts we bring; all that we have is Yours alone, a trust from You, our King!" In Jesus' name. Amen.

Trustees!
People with a Purpose!

In this session we will endeavor to

*grow in understanding that trustees are to bear in mind
the purposes of the owner as we manage affairs for Him;*

*become more aware of God's purposes
for the resources He has entrusted to us;*

*expand our ability to manage the resources
God has entrusted to us.*

Opening Prayer

Psalm 100

*O Lord God, Father, Son, and Holy Spirit—give us Your
wisdom as we grow together in the sharing of Your Word.
Enlighten our minds and hearts, O Holy Spirit, so that we can
discern Your will and fulfill Your purposes in our daily lives. We
rejoice in the privilege of being called as Your trustees. Enable
us, O Lord, to serve You with confidence, perseverance, and joy-
ful spirits. In Jesus' name we pray. Amen.*

Seeking Wisdom . . .

When a person serves as a manager of a chain store, she is
expected to manage her store in keeping with company policies
and purposes. The company entrusts her with authority to make
decisions that will help that branch operation further the company's goals.

In a similar way, God's purposes apply to His people. God
sets out His plan and purpose. He gives His people freedom to
carry out their responsibilities. The Owner's goals and intentions

continually shape and mold people's attitude, decision-making, and action.

Read Genesis 1:26–28 and 2:15–17. The Creator places people into the world as His representatives to take care of what belongs to Him. This responsibility extends to all people, whether they are conscious of their creation by God or not. God's purposes are universally applicable. Responsibility is involved, and to some extent nature and conscience reveal that. We find a helpful summary of God's purposes in the Ten Commandments, especially in what is called "the second table of God's Law."

Consider the following references and questions for discussing God's universally applicable purposes.

31. Read Exodus 20:12; Deuteronomy 5:16; Ephesians 6:1–4; and Romans 13:1–7. The Fourth Commandment reads "Honor your father and mother." Family and government, part of the created order, are gifts of God. What stewardship responsibilities rest upon parents? Children? What is the role of the governed? The government?

32. Read Exodus 20:13; Deuteronomy 5:17; and 1 Corinthians 3:16; 6:19. The Fifth Commandment reads,"You shall not kill (commit murder)." God gives life and desires to protect and nurture life. What can you do for your own body to respond to the high value God places on the gift of life? What are a trustee's responsibilities in caring for the life of others? What illustrations show how this is currently being done? Example: World Relief, community action, and so on.

33. Read Exodus 20:13; Deuteronomy 5:18; Hebrews 13:4; and 1 Thessalonians 4:3–6. The Sixth Commandment reads "You shall not commit adultery." God made male and female (Genesis 1:27). God declared His creation "good." What are God's purposes for sex? How do God's purposes instruct our sexual conduct and shape our stewardship of our maleness or femaleness? Read 1 Corinthians 6:12–20 for additional insight.

34. Read Exodus 20:15; Deuteronomy 5:19; and Ephesians 4:28. The Seventh Commandment reads, "You shall not steal." In this commandment God shows His concern for property, livelihood, and caring for others as part of our trusteeship within the created order. What does He desire we do and not do to be His stewards regarding property, business, work, talents, needs of others, and so forth?

35. Read Exodus 20:16; Deuteronomy 5:20; Proverbs 22:1; and James 3:2–12. The Eighth Commandment reads, "You shall not bear false witness against your neighbor." A name and a good reputation are among God's best gifts to people, but the stewardship of this gift appears to be one of the most difficult to manage. What positive benefits result from the control and God-pleasing use of the tongue? What negatives result from not controlling the tongue?

36. Read Exodus 20:17; Deuteronomy 5:21; Matthew 15:19; Luke 12:15; and Colossians 3:5–8. The Ninth and Tenth Commandments read, "You shall not covet . . . ." These commandments involve the stewardship of the heart, the mind, and the will. Consider Romans 7:7 and the story of Naboth's vineyard (1 Kings 21) as illustrations of the consequences of coveting, and consider the truth of Jesus' words in Matthew 15:19. How do these commandments relate to the Sixth and Seventh Commandments? Coveting turns the steward-owner relationship upside down!

Reflecting . . .

If we stopped after examining our stewardship/trusteeship in the light of the above Scriptures... well, we'd likely despair! What gives hope to all stewards is that there is One perfect steward, Jesus, God's Son, Savior of all, who exercised His trust responsibly, wisely, and well . . . and He did it on behalf of all of us, all God's stewards!

As we consider John 3:16; Galatians 4:4–7; Romans 3:21–26; Luke 2:51; John 19:27; Matthew 22:16; and 1 Peter 2:21–24, we discover some really good news! Jesus honored His parents, cared for a dying mother, healed the sick, restored the dead to life, spoke the truth to friend and foe alike, and acted out the ultimate stewardship test by enduring false accusation and even death. In all of this He trusted His Father to the end and fulfilled His purpose: not to be served, but to serve, and to give His life as a ransom for many (Mark 10:45; 1 Peter 2:21–24). His rising from death to life on the third day is the sign that His stewardship was perfect and complete (Matthew 28:1–7; Luke 24:4–8; 1 Corinthians 15:1–22).

This Good News means that what Jesus Christ did was done for you and me, for all! He gives us freedom from fear about the future, our health, our death. He also gives us the freedom to be His stewards, trustees, managers, caregivers, agents, administrators, who live as children of God (1 John 3:1–3; Colossians 3:1–4; 2 Corinthians 5:14–15), His representatives and reflectors of His image in this world.

The church is called "the body of Christ" (1 Corinthians 12:12–13, 27; Romans 12:3–5) and is made up of all those who trust in Christ as Savior and Lord. Such faith involves a special privilege and responsibility (ability to respond!) that goes beyond the created order. No one else has been given this stewardship. It is given only to those who know and believe that Jesus Christ is the One who restores us to a right relationship with our Creator. He entrusts His mission and purpose to us!

Reflect on the following Bible portions and put in your own words the special mission, purpose, stewardship, that God has given to followers of Jesus Christ.

37. 1 Peter 2:4–12. Note how Peter lifts up both the speaking and doing functions for God's people. What are they? What is the content of their speaking? Why are both roles critically important? What light does "the day of visitation" shed on this question?

38. Matthew 28:16–20. This section is often called "The Great Commission." Jesus' central instruction here is "as you go about your life, make disciples, baptizing and teaching them." Verse 18 indicates the authority by which we carry out this stewardship. What does "therefore" (v. 19) encompass? What is the basis of the church's distinctive purpose? Look up 2 Corinthians 5:14–15 and Titus 2:11–14 and reflect on them in the light of Matthew 28. What does this stir inside you?

39. Luke 19:11–27. The "parable of the pounds" is very similar to the parable of the talents. In view of the context and the previous story about Zacchaeus, we understand this parable to refer to the church's stewardship of the Gospel (individually and corporately). In what way can the church "trade with these until I come" (v. 13, RSV)? How does a believer or a congregation "trade with the Gospel"? How does a believer or a congregation invest the Gospel to fulfill the Owner's intention?

Applying . . . Living What We Believe . . .

How can I carry out the church's mission personally? This is a critical question, because if I do not respond, who will? The church as an institution will get nothing done if its individual members do not respond to the privilege of being God's steward . . . stewards of the Gospel! Institutions and organizations only have as much influence as the individuals who make them up. Since this is true, consider the following Bible passages as part of growing and developing attitudes, gifts, and skills as God's trustee.

40. My relationship with my Lord. Read and meditate on Ephesians 6:10–20; Matthew 9:35–38; 2 Thessalonians 3:1–2; and Colossians 4:2–6. What have you discovered?

41. My relationship with other people. Read and meditate on Matthew 5:14–16; John 8:12; Acts 8:35 and 13:47; 1 Thessalonians 5:11 and 19–22; and 1 Corinthians 3:6–9. How is God working through you?

42. My management of talents, gifts, and skills for the health of the church. Read and meditate on Romans 12:3–8; 1 Peter 4:7–11; and 1 Corinthians 12:7. Whose lives am I touching? How? How is it going?

43. My management of God's financial resources for the spread of the Gospel. Read and meditate on Romans 15:23–33; Philippians 4:10–19; Luke 12:32–34; 1 Corinthians 16:1–2; and 1 Timothy 6:17–19. What is the plan being followed? Could it be updated? When? How?

Until Next Time . . .

Why is it critical for the church to fulfill her mission? Consider John 14:6 and Acts 4:12. There is only one sure way for people to be put right with God now and eternally! Jesus Christ, His Son, Savior of the world, is the bridge God gave to bring people to Himself. He entrusts us with the life-giving message of hope for all people. We are privileged to be His witnesses, stewards, trustees (Acts 1:8; Isaiah 43:1–3a, 10–12; 1 Peter

2:9–10; Ephesians 2:8–10), bringing light, life, and love to all whose lives we can touch.

Who has touched your life with the forgiving grace and love of Christ? Whose life will you be privileged to touch in the days ahead? Pray, reflect, make a plan. You're His trustee, chosen for His purpose!

Summarizing . . .

• God reveals His purposes in the created order.
• God calls His church into being for His special mission.
• God works through His people to reach other people with the life-changing message of Jesus.
• God's Holy Spirit enables me/us to fulfill His purposes.

Closing Prayer

Heavenly Father, maker and owner of all that is, Your glory fills the world. We have seen Your glory in the face of Jesus Christ. He is the Chief Steward, who fulfilled His stewardship perfectly so that we could be Your stewards now and forever. O Lord, use us as Your instrument to bless, encourage, and nurture the people to whom You send us each day. Empower us with Your Spirit's wisdom and energy. Help us recognize the opportunities You give us to be stewards of the Gospel each day. In Jesus' name we pray. Amen.

Trusting
and
Trustworthy!

In this session we will endeavor to

affirm again that God can be trusted, that He is faithful;

*understand that God desires His trustees, stewards,
to be trustworthy, faithful;*

*realize that God calls us to take risks for Him,
to trust Him in serving;*

*grow in ability to live a life of faith
and faithfulness.*

Opening Prayer

Proverbs 3:1–10

*O Lord God—Father, Son, and Holy Spirit—bless us with
an abundance of Your Holy Spirit. In the middle of the doubts,
fears, and struggles of life, help us to remember Your faithfulness revealed in Jesus, our Lord. Help us to trust Your promises
and respond with a life of continuing faithfulness to your purposes. In Jesus' name we pray. Amen.*

Seeking Wisdom . . .

Read again Matthew 25:14–30. Take a new look at the
basis for the evaluation of the stewardship attitudes and prac-
tices of the three trustees.

44. What does the master highlight at the report of the
"five talent" man (v. 21)? What is said of the second trustee (v.

23)? In contrast, what does the "one talent" man admit in his report (vv. 24–28)? What causes his action?

45. What helps remove the fear that can cripple one's stewardship and replace it with a willingness to risk, to dare good things for our Lord's purposes?

46. Read Luke 16:10–13. The context (vv. 1–9) indicates that the "very little" to be faithful with is money. How can we be helpful to one another in managing money? What guides us in the way it is saved, spent, used, invested?

47. How do our decisions about money reflect that we are God's representatives (as discussed in the previous session)? How might we allot His money to fulfill His purposes? How might these decisions change over the course of life with Christ?

48. In Matthew 25, the third trustee buried the money because he was afraid. What does that say about his view of the master? What is the relationship between faith and fear? Are they compatible?

49. On U.S. currency it says, "In God we trust." Give some illustrations of trust in daily life experiences. How is trust shown?

50. Consider Malachi 3:6–12. While we, by God's grace in Christ, do not live under the Law (Romans 6:14; 7:4–6; Colossians 2:16–17), what is the principle that God appeals to in the text? What were the priests and people doing with their offerings (see Malachi 1:6–14)? What did they bring to God?

51. Ever since the fall into sin, trusting God has not been easy for human beings. Our innate tendency is to rely on our own self and do what *we* think is right and best. Read 2 Corinthians 9:6–15 and identify the promises that help put fear to rest and awaken faith. Share your insights with the group. How did

God's people in Corinth resist the pressures of culture and grow as faith-full stewards?

52. Mark 12:41–44 is a unique illustration. When it comes to money management, it may seem like the poor widow is a poor example. Read aloud the brief story. What did she do? What would she have to live on now? What does Jesus say? Why does He hold her up as an example to others who were listening?

Reflecting . . .

Let the faithfulness of God inspire your own faithfulness! It is true: the key to our faithfulness as Jesus' followers, trustees, stewards, is God's faithfulness. God is trustworthy. The Bible is the account of that trust from Genesis to Revelation. The ministry of God's Son, Jesus, is the core of that faithfulness.

53. Read 2 Timothy 2:11–13. It sounds like a baptismal hymn. What resounding affirmation concludes the song? How does remembering our own Baptism and God's promises there nurture our trust?

54. Recall some of God's promises from memory. Share them with the group. Tell of a Christian friend, neighbor, parent, child, or spouse who has been an example of trust in God and trustworthiness in life. What has been learned from him or her?

55. Think of three people you would trust, and tell about the qualities they exhibit that encourage you or that you would like to develop.

As you share together, have volunteers read aloud these Bible passages for the group: 1 Thessalonians 5:24; 1 Corinthians 1:4–9; 10:6–13; and 1 Peter 4:19. As a group, scan 1 Corinthians 15, the great resurrection chapter, and notice how the resurrection of Jesus Christ from the dead is the power for godly living (especially note v. 58).

56. When planning a budget, does it make a difference what you put first? Why?

57. Attitude is an important aspect of stewardship. 2 Corinthians 9:7 says, "God loves a cheerful giver." The original word for cheerful is "hilarious"! Who are the "hilarious" stewards in your congregation? Among your acquaintances? What are they like? How would you describe them to a newspaper reporter?

Applying . . . Living What We Believe . . .

58. Who do you know that seems to really "get a bang out of giving," out of showing generosity in the management of money for the Lord's purposes? How did he or she develop that type of attitude and practice? Who helped him or her?

59. Was there a time or situation when you had an attitude of generosity because of something you did or a project you supported? Can you describe the experience, the sensation, the realization that you were "God's trustee"?

60. Lutheran pastor Charles Mueller, Sr., frequently says, "I never met an ex-tither!" What does that mean? What joys, satisfactions, sense of meaning have you discovered when giving generously for a cause that you know is "of God"? Can you describe the process, the feeling involved?

61. An examination of the ledger in the personal or family checkbook is one of the ways some stewards have begun the process of personal or family evaluation of their stewardship. What does that process reveal? How might it cause great joy among a household of "God's trustees"? What difference might that make in the budgeting, management, and stewarding processes?

62. What application does 2 Corinthians 8:1–9 have for you? Your household? Your congregation?

Until Next Time . . .

God's Word emphasizes that faithfulness flows from faith. Hebrews 11:6 says, "Without faith it is impossible to please God." The person who trusts can be a trustworthy steward. The right relationship with God that faith in Jesus Christ receives enables us to grow in the ability to administer one's resources faithfully.

Picture this: All of God's resources given to you are like the contents of a large warehouse. There is a great variety inside. Our privilege is to receive, discover, develop, distribute, and manage—for the blessing of others (and our self-care too)—what God has put into the particular "warehouse" He has loaned to us. What are the joys you have discovered in managing "God's warehouse"? Tell a friend! Tell the Lord too!

Summarizing . . .

- God is faithful. He keeps His promises.
- God trusts His trustees.
- God invites us to put Him first, to risk setting priorities that reveal "God comes first."
- God stands with us as we continue to grow in wisdom and skill to be God's trustees.

Closing Prayer

I am trusting You, Lord Jesus,
Trusting only You;
Trusting You for full salvation,
Free and true.

I am trusting You to guide me;
You alone shall lead,
Ev'ry day and hour supplying
All my need.

I am trusting You for power;
You can never fail.

Words which You Yourself shall give me
Must prevail.

I am trusting You, Lord Jesus;
Never let me fall.
I am trusting You forever
And for all. Amen! (*LW* 408)

Trustees, Let Love Shine Through!

In this session we will endeavor to

*discover that our stewardship is a way for us
to reflect the character and essential quality
of our Lord and Owner: LOVE;*

*express our love for the One who has created
and redeemed us, giving us the privilege
of being His managers, trustees;*

be encouraged to keep our love alive and growing.

Opening Prayer

1 John 4:7–16

*O Lord God—Father, Son, and Holy Spirit—ignite in our
hearts the renewing fire of Your love. Shape and fashion our
hearts and minds, O God, so that in accord with Your will we
may be the instruments of Your goodness to serve all those to
whom You send us, far and near. In Jesus' name we pray. Amen.*

Seeking Wisdom . . .

As God's trustees we are called to use faithfully the
resources God has entrusted to us. In previous sessions we discussed how we grow in using those resources according to the
will of the Owner (the One who provides the "warehouse" and
the variety within it). There is another important dimension to
what our stewardship is all about. It has to do with our call to
reflect the character, personality, and qualities of the Owner! It
is a great calling . . . and a great trust!

As highlighted in the opening reading and prayer, the trait
that leaps from the pages of Holy Scripture is LOVE! In Jesus

Christ we see God revealed as the God who *loves* His people. Because "God is love" (1 John 4:16), we who are His stewards, trustees, are empowered to love.

63. Read aloud Mark 14:3–9. This certainly is an extravagant act! Nard was very costly, a precious perfume imported from India. One denarius was one day's wage. 300 denarii would be the equivalent of a full year's wages! Some people believe the action was excessive. What do you think? What would lead a person to expend so many of her resources in such a way? What practical results were achieved by what this woman did?

64. Jesus defends the woman's generous action. "She has done a beautiful thing to Me" (v. 6), He says in the face of the criticism leveled against her. Can you describe the scene and the feelings it may have generated? What does Jesus say about the appropriateness of her actions (vv. 6–9)?

65. Stewards can miss opportunities to serve, even extravagantly. Jesus was not going to be present much longer. Perhaps the woman sensed this. Read verse 3 again. Where did this generosity take place? In whose house? See Mark 1:40–45 and Leviticus 13:45–46. What had the woman likely received? What did she give in response?

66. Read Luke 7:36–50. This is a similar story, but perhaps not the same one. Notice how Jesus helped the people there understand the woman's motive by the illustration in verses 41–42. What's the point? Why did the woman do it? See 1 John 4:19. Please share some examples of the extravagance of love that you have heard of or known personally.

Experiencing the love of God revealed in Jesus Christ makes a growing difference in the use of the variety of resources that God has entrusted to us. The following are just a few of the broad categories that trustees have to "let the Son shine through."

67. Our body. Good stewards will take care of their body. What does the psalmist (Psalm 139:13–14) admit about himself, about his mind and his accomplishments? See also 1 Corinthians 6:19–20.

68. The "stuff" of the world we can enjoy. Consider some of the processes and people involved in enabling a person to enjoy a loaf of freshly baked bread. What does the psalmist confess about his blessings, even his daily bread (Psalm 103:1–5; Psalm 145:15–16)?

69. The gift of resources we hold in common with others: the world around us (Psalm 24:1; 89:11), public property, water, air, parks, schools, and the like. Romans 13:1 tells us where government—which is involved in many of these jointly held trusts—fits in. The psalmist reminds us of the source of these gifts. Why has He provided them?

70. The gift of other people. The comment is sometimes made that even our children are "on loan" to us. Consider the story of Hannah in 1 Samuel 1:5, 11, and 20–28. See also Psalm 127:3. How are others a gift from God?

71. The gift of the Gospel—the spoken Word, the written Word, or the visible Word in the Sacraments. Consider John 1:14–18; Romans 3:21–28; and Galatians 4:4–7. What do you consider the most meaningful aspect of the Gospel for your life?

72. The gift of time—the psalmist says, "My times are in Your hands!" (Psalm 31:15). Isaac Watt teaches us to sing, "On Thee each moment we depend; if Thou withdraw, we die." How does an awareness of the gift of time influence our reflection of the love of God the Giver?

73. Even a quick review of these resources will help us discover what Jacob confessed when he prepared to meet his brother Esau in Genesis 32:9–12. Remember that he had tricked his
brother and now was preparing to meet him. What helped him
make this confession? What was his main emotion? Can we
reflect a Jacob-like gratitude without having to be confronted
with the possibility of our death (or someone else's)? What or
who can help us see that the resources we have are a result of
God's undeserved love?

Applying . . . Living What We Believe . . .

God's love is not a theory. "God demonstrates His own love
for us in this: While we were still sinners, Christ died for us."
(Romans 5:8). This love is extravagant. Consider the story of the
waiting father in Luke 15:11–31. This surely is extravagant love
. . . given again, even in the face of disappointment and waste!

1 John 3:16–18 ties God's love together with our response
in very practical and applicable ways. It reminds us of Jesus'
words to His trustees in Matthew 5:43–48 and in John 13:34–35.

74. As a group, try to put into a few sentences or paragraphs a summary that will challenge each one of you to grow in
reflecting back to God His kind of love. What does this love
look like? Where does it begin? Does it start at home? How is it
extended into the community? In the congregation? Among
those who are "different" from us?

75. Share some examples of how you have seen the love of God grow and be reflected among the members of the congregation or in the group with whom you are now meeting. Do not be shy in sharing the stories of Christ's life-transforming love. It's part of being a steward of a great gift from God!

76. The above activity is important to the individual and corporate stewardship of God's love. Read 2 Timothy 3:1–5; Matthew 24:12; and Philippians 2:14–16. Notice the commentary on the culture in which Paul lived. Note the contrast of being God's loving stewards, "shining like stars" in the middle of dark and stormy surroundings! What can help us "keep our love at full strength" (1 Peter 4:8, NEB)? Who do you know that "lets the sun (Son) shine through" in an encouraging fashion, no matter what the circumstance? Describe that person. What is God doing through that love?

Until Next Time . . .

What are some of the "little things" that people do that soon add up to a big bundle of love for the other person? Have you ever been on the receiving end of those "little things"? Could you make a list of them and tell the giver about them and how they reflected the love of Christ to you? It's a part of being God's trustee!

In what ways are you on the giving end of those "little things" that, put together, make up the bigger picture and mirror the love of Christ to others? Don't be shy. Remember that "God . . . works in you to will and to act according to His good purpose" (Philippians 2:13).

Summarizing. . .

- God's love is extravagant. He is reflected in the growing Christlike lives of His stewards.
- It is a continuing challenge and privilege to express in word and deed our Redeemer's love.
- We help each other in our family and the family of God to grow in "letting the sun (Son) shine through."

Closing Prayer

O Lord God, Father, Son, and Holy Spirit—hear us as we pray:

When I survey the wondrous cross
On which the Prince of glory died,
My richest gain I count but loss
And pour contempt on all my pride.

Forbid it, Lord, that I should boast
Save in the death of Christ, my God;
All the vain things that charm me most,
I sacrifice them to His blood.

See, from His head, His hands, His feet
Sorrow and love flow mingled down.
Did e'er such love and sorrow meet
Or thorns compose so rich a crown?

Were the whole realm of nature mine,
That were a tribute far too small;
Love so amazing, so divine,
Demands my soul, my life, my all! (*LW* 115)

To God Be the Glory!

In this session we will endeavor to

discover what it means to give glory to God
through our daily stewardship;
encourage each other to live a life that glorifies God
in word and deed;
realize that our present stewardship is a foretaste
of our glorifying of God forever in heaven.

Opening Prayer

Psalm 145:1–13

O Lord God, Father, Son, and Holy Spirit—Giver of every good and of all that we are and have—bless us with Your wisdom, presence, and peace. Help us to glorify You in our stewardship of life. Shape our attitudes and actions so that those around us will know that we belong to You and that You have made us Your trustees, now and forever. In Jesus' name we pray. Amen.

Seeking Wisdom . . .

Ever since the ascension of Jesus (Luke 24; Acts 1), His followers have lived in anticipation of the end of the world and His return, or the end of their life in this world and His summons to be with Him forever. This reality gives our stewardship a present and eternal dimension. That truth is reflected in many places in the Bible.

77. To gain wisdom from God's Word, read aloud 1 Peter 4:7–11. "Giving glory to God" may include singing uplifting

songs of praise, offering prayers of thanksgiving, and the like. However, it is more than that. What is involved in God's trustees glorifying God?

78. What is the significance of verses 7 and 8? What do they bring to mind for the situation in your life and your congregation? Please put those two verses into your own summary and share them with the group. How could this practice be a blessing to others *and* glorify God?

79. Please take a close look at verses 10–11. Read them in a variety of translations. What is the congregational nature of the gifts we have received from God as individuals? See 1 Corinthians 12:7 in this connection. Notice that only two gifts are mentioned in 1 Peter 4:7–11 . . . *speaking* and *serving*. These are "umbrella-like" categories of gifts, talents, or skills that God provides. How do these categories illustrate the truth that God does not give us an assignment (a stewardship) without also giving us the resources to fulfill it?

80. Consulting the following passages can enable us to see how stewards, trustees of opportunities, can give glory to God through our *speaking*: John 12:49–50; 2 Corinthians 2:17; and Ephesians 4:25, 29–32. Note what you learn.

81. Examining the following passages can enable us to see how we can give glory to God through the stewardship of our *serving*: Romans 12:1–2, 6–8; Galatians 5:13–15 and 6:7–10; and 1 Thessalonians 4:1–2, 9–12.

82. As a group, make a list to help one another realize and recognize the gifts that are currently being used and shared by the people in the congregation. What do they include? After you do that, also consider Romans 12:3–8; 1 Corinthians 12:4–12; and Ephesians 4:11–16.

83. How would you describe *the purpose* of all these gifts, talents, skills, and resources that God provides? What happens because of them? How does that give glory to God?

84. Check out 1 Corinthians 10:31–11:1 and notice what Paul writes about stewards giving glory to God. What does it include? Please note that the wider context is 1 Corinthians 8:1–11:1 and the specific example from Paul's life.

85. See Romans 4:19–22. In what sense is Abraham giving glory to God?

86. A story of what happens with the *abuse* of one's position is found in Acts 12:1–3, 18–23. What was the outcome for Herod? Why? See verse 23.

87. 2 Corinthians 9:6–15 is a remarkable story. It shows how the monetary gifts of God's stewards in Corinth became the seedlings that resulted in others glorifying God. Take special note of verses 11–13. Have you seen anything like that happen in or through your congregation or church body? Please share your stories!

Reflecting . . .

God's trustees are like dispensers. God fills and refills our lives with His blessings, talents, skills, and gifts. We are asked, privileged by the Owner, to dispense those gifts to others in the name of our Lord.

In our society the "bottom line" is often profitability, success, power, control, and/or "what's in it for me?"! For the steward, it is *honoring God*, going God's way, following God's direction, because life itself is seen as belonging to the One who created and redeemed us: Jesus, God's Son, our Savior and Lord! Because of the depth of His mercy, love, and kindness (2 Corinthians 5:14–15 and 8:9; Ephesians 2:8–10; Titus 2:11–14), God's trustees look differently at life. Stewards seek to serve the Lord by serving other people!

88. What helps us go "against the grain" of the world and its self-seeking, self-satisfying focus? What empowers us to resist the temptation to usurp God's role and instead continue to be trustees on behalf of our Lord?

89. Reflect on 1 Peter 4:12–19 and/or 1 Peter 1:3–7. What thoughts in these paragraphs can strengthen God's stewards to *"glorify God in all things"* even while enduring hardship or suffering?

90. Can you think of some people God put into your life who exemplify that level of trusteeship? What did they do? What are they like? (If time permits, perhaps 1 Peter 2:9–12 will be of help.)

Applying . . . Living What We Believe . . .

In Luke 10:17–20 the disciples return from the stewardship mission of sharing the truth as it is in Jesus. They most likely saw great changes in some people's lives (vv. 1–16). Notice what Jesus says is the ultimate reason for rejoicing as God's stewards!

91. In Philippians 4:10–20 St. Paul shares his trust in our Lord and also his thanks for the partnership he had with the stewards from that congregation. Share some of the "stewardship partnerships" in which individuals or the whole congregation have been involved. What were the results? Who received the benefits? How did this partnership glorify God?

92. In summarizing the things shared as God's trustees, consider reading the insights of the apostle Paul in Ephesians 1:3–12 and 15–19; Colossians 1:9–14; or 1 Thessalonians 1:2–10. Each section aids our understanding of the privilege of being called to be God's stewards!

93. What will be the same, different, or changed in our lives, in our witness to others in the congregation, community, and the church-at-large, as a result of our study of Christian stewardship and our being God's trustees?

Summarizing . . .

• Giving glory to God is more than songs of praise or occasional prayers.
• Giving glory to God is corporate, using each believer's gift to assist fellow stewards.
• Giving glory to God takes place in the here and now . . . and will continue forever!

    Being God's trustee and steward is an honor and privilege. It comes from God. It is not self-generated. God trusts His believing people to manage life and all life's resources for Him (session 1). Our Creator provides the resources that enable us to fulfill His call to trusteeship (session 2). We are guided in the exercise of this trust by the purposes He set forth for people in creation and revealed in Scripture for the specific mission of the church (session 3). God's desire for all His stewards is faithfulness in using His resources freely and generously for His purposes (session 4). His stewards seek to reflect His qualities and characteristics, radiating His love through our stewardship (session 5). Living in the light of the cross of Christ, as stewards of all of life and life's resources, we give glory to God in all we are, say, and do. Jesus is our Lord, and we are privileged to join in the theme song of a fellow steward, the apostle Paul (Romans 11:36): ". . . from Him and through Him and to Him are all things! To Him be glory forever! Amen."

Closing Prayer

Direct us, O Lord, with Your most gracious favor. In all of life, support us with Your continual help so that all our stewardship, begun, continued, and ended in You, may glorify Your holy name, fulfill Your good and gracious will, and fill earth and heaven with Your praise! In Jesus' name we pray. Amen.

Placing the Blessing upon God's Trustees

"May the God of peace, who through the blood of the eternal covenant brought back from the dead our Lord Jesus, that great Shepherd of the sheep, equip you with everything good for doing His will, and may He work in us what is pleasing to Him, through Jesus Christ; to whom be glory for ever and ever. Amen." (Hebrews 13:20–21)

Go in peace. Be God's stewards!

Response: Thanks be to God!